D1064576

CHECKERBOARD BIOGRAPHIES

MELANIA TRUMP

RACHAEL L. THOMAS

Checkerboard
Library

An Imprint of Abdo Publishing
abdobooks.com

ABDOBOOKS.COM

Published by Abdo Publishing, a division of ABDO, PO Box 398166, Minneapolis, Minnesota 55439.
Copyright © 2020 by Abdo Consulting Group, Inc. International copyrights reserved in all countries.
No part of this book may be reproduced in any form without written permission from the publisher.
Checkerboard Library™ is a trademark and logo of Abdo Publishing.

Printed in the United States of America, North Mankato, Minnesota
052019
092019

THIS BOOK CONTAINS
RECYCLED MATERIALS

Design and Production: Mighty Media, Inc.
Editor: Megan Borgert-Spaniol
Cover Photograph: Library of Congress
Interior Photographs: AP Images, pp. 7, 23, 29 (bottom right); Shutterstock Images, pp. 5, 11, 13, 15, 19, 25, 28 (all), 29 (top, bottom left); The White House/Flickr, pp. 9, 18, 21, 27; The White House/Wikimedia Commons, p. 17

Library of Congress Control Number: 2018966245

Publisher's Cataloging-in-Publication Data
Names: Thomas, Rachael L., author.
Title: Melania Trump / by Rachael L. Thomas
Description: Minneapolis, Minnesota : Abdo Publishing, 2020 | Series: Checkerboard biographies |
    Includes online resources and index.
Identifiers: ISBN 9781532119408 (lib. bdg.) | ISBN 9781532173868 (ebook.)
Subjects: LCSH: Trump, Melania, 1970- --Juvenile literature. | First ladies (United States)--Biography--
    Juvenile literature. | Fashion models--Biography--Juvenile literature. | Women entrepreneurs--
    Biography--Juvenile literature.
Classification: DDC 973.933092 [B]--dc23

CONTENTS

CHAPTER 1

FOREIGN-BORN FIRST LADY

Melania Trump is best known for her role as First Lady of the United States alongside her husband, President Donald Trump. In this role, she became a well-known political figure. However, Trump is also known for her previous career in modeling and fashion.

Trump began her career as a fashion model when she was a teenager in Eastern Europe. She **immigrated** to the United States to pursue opportunities in the industry. Before becoming First Lady, Trump worked as a successful model and fashion designer.

 No one values the freedom and opportunity of America more than me, both as an independent woman, and as someone who immigrated to America.

As First Lady, Trump launched a campaign to promote healthy lifestyles for children. Her belief in children's social and emotional education has helped people across America and beyond.

Trump is a private person. As First Lady, she was known for her quiet manner and rare public appearances.

CHAPTER 2

INTERNATIONAL DREAMS

Melanija Knavs was born in what is now the central European country of Slovenia on April 26, 1970. She later changed her name to Melania Knauss. While her birthplace was a town called Novo Mesto, Melania grew up in the nearby town of Sevnica. She has one older sister, Ines.

Melania's parents are Amalija and Viktor Knavs. Viktor traveled as a car dealer. Amalija worked in a **textile** factory. She designed patterns for the clothes that were made at the factory. Melania says her first experience modeling was at five years old when she modeled the textile factory's designs.

When Melania was growing up, Slovenia was part of the **communist** country Yugoslavia. Yugoslavia experienced serious political unrest during Melania's childhood. But Melania was largely shielded from this **upheaval**. Her family was well off, and her dreams went

Viktor and Amalija Knavs became US citizens in August 2018.

beyond her home country. Melania had inherited her
mother's interest in fashion. She dreamed of moving
abroad and having a career in fashion and design.

CHAPTER 3

INTERNATIONAL CONTRACT

As a teenager, Melania often attended fashion shows. In 1987, she attended a show in Slovenia's capital city, Ljubljana. There, photographer Stane Jerko caught sight of her. Jerko asked Melania if she would model for him, and Melania agreed.

Over the next few years, Melania took on more modeling jobs. She also concentrated on school. Melania began studying **architecture** and design at the University of Ljubljana. But modeling would soon become her **priority**.

In 1992, the Slovenian magazine *Jana* launched the Look of the Year Contest. The contest aimed to provide modeling opportunities to Slovenian women. The top three contestants would win international modeling contracts.

Melania entered the Look of the Year Contest and came in second place. Her prize was a modeling contract in Milan, Italy. Melania discontinued her university studies to move to Milan. She was focused on her goal to become an international supermodel.

Melania's modeling experience prepared her for the many photos she would pose for as First Lady of the United States.

MODEL NEW YORKER

After leaving school, Knauss spent the next few years working as a model in Milan and Paris, France. By 1996, she had caught the attention of US-based modeling agent Paolo Zampolli. Knauss moved to New York City that same year, after being signed by Zampolli's agency, ID Models.

Knauss lived a **disciplined** life in New York. She didn't stay out late at parties and night clubs like many others in her industry. She looked after her body by eating a healthy diet and exercising. Knauss was serious about her career and worked hard to maintain it.

In 1998, Knauss attended a party thrown by Zampolli. Attending the event was businessman Donald Trump. Knauss and Donald met that night, and Donald asked Knauss for her number. But instead of giving away her number, Knauss asked to take Donald's number. A week later, she called him.

It's very important to take care of yourself. Once you take care of yourself, you can take care of other people.

When Knauss met Donald, Donald was a widely known businessman. Several years later, he would become famous for his role on the reality TV show *The Apprentice*.

CHAPTER 5

FROM KNAUSS TO TRUMP

After they met, Knauss and Donald dated on and off for seven years. During this time, Knauss achieved more success in modeling.

In 2001, Knauss moved into Trump Tower on Fifth Avenue in New York City. Trump Tower was the **skyscraper** where Donald lived and held his business headquarters. The following year, the couple visited Knauss's home country together. There, Donald met Knauss's parents.

In January 2005, Knauss and Donald married. The couple hosted a large wedding ceremony in Palm Beach, Florida. There were more than 350 guests at Knauss and Donald's wedding. Donald wanted the wedding to be filmed and aired live, but Knauss refused. This desire for privacy would define her future manner as First Lady.

DRESSED FOR SUCCESS

Melania Trump's wedding dress weighed 60 pounds (27 kg) and cost $100,000. At the time, it was the most expensive wedding dress in history!

Melania and Donald lived in the top three floors of Trump Tower.

Once married, Knauss changed her last name to Knauss-Trump. Eventually, she would go by Melania Trump. In September 2005, news broke that Trump was pregnant with her and Donald's first child.

Trump gave birth to a son, Barron, in March 2006. That same year, she became a US citizen. For the next few years, Trump worked as a full-time mother.

Once Barron started school, Trump continued to pursue her interests in fashion and design. In 2010, Trump launched her own jewelry collection, Melania Timepieces & Jewelry. All 13,500 items in the **initial** collection sold out within 45 minutes of the launch!

With her jewelry collection, Trump had proven to be a successful **entrepreneur**. But this period of Trump's career would soon end. In June 2015, her husband announced that he would be running for President of the United States. Trump didn't know it, but she was about to become the nation's First Lady.

FINE INGREDIENTS

Trump launched a skincare line in 2013. The collection used caviar, or fish eggs, as a main ingredient!

Barron Trump (*middle*) is the youngest of Donald Trump's children. Eric (*left*), Ivanka (*second from right*), Donald Jr. (*right*), and Tiffany (*not pictured*) are Barron's half-siblings.

CHAPTER 6

THE WHITE HOUSE

After Donald announced his presidential candidacy, he campaigned across America. Trump mostly supported her husband from home as he traveled from state to state. When she joined him, she gave speeches expressing her faith in her husband's skills and values.

On November 9, 2016, Donald won the presidential election against competitor Hillary Clinton. Two months later, he was sworn in as president. Trump was the nation's new First Lady.

Donald moved to the White House after his **inauguration** in January 2017. But Trump did not move to Washington, DC, with her husband right away. Instead, she and Barron stayed in New York while Barron completed the school year.

MULTILINGUAL MELANIA

Trump was an uncommon First Lady. She was the first in almost 200 years to have been born outside the United States. She was also the first whose native language wasn't English. In fact, Trump speaks six languages, including Slovenian, French, and German. This is more languages than any First Lady, or president, before her could speak!

The only other foreign-born First Lady was Louisa Adams. Adams was English. She was married to President John Quincy Adams and was First Lady from 1825 to 1829.

Even as First Lady, Trump often stated that her son was her first **priority**. Barron was ten years old when his family entered the White House. Trump wanted Barron to have as normal a childhood as possible. She also wanted to protect Barron from the national spotlight and any **negative** media attention.

In June 2017, Trump and Barron moved from New York City into the White House in Washington, DC. A new life in the nation's capital would bring projects and responsibilities for the whole family.

BIO BASICS

NAME: Melania Trump

BIRTH: April 26, 1970, Novo Mesto, Yugoslavia (now Slovenia)

SPOUSE: Donald Trump (2005-present)

CHILD: Barron

FAMOUS FOR: her role as First Lady of the United States as of 2017; her career as an international model and fashion designer

ACHIEVEMENTS: launched the successful jewelry collection Melania Timepieces & Jewelry; launched the Be Best campaign to help develop children's social and emotional health

CHAPTER 7

ANTI-BULLYING CAMPAIGN

The First Lady of the United States is an important figure. Historically, individuals in this role have used their influence to make positive changes in the country and world. In November 2016, Trump made a speech in Philadelphia, Pennsylvania. She announced that as First Lady, she would work to prevent cyberbullying.

Cyberbullying is when people **intimidate**, mock, or **demoralize** others online. It often happens on social media platforms. Trump talked about how children and teenagers can suffer emotionally from online bullying.

Once Trump was settled at her White House residence, her mission expanded. She wanted to address bullying in schools too. In October 2017, Trump made a surprise visit to a middle school in Michigan. She was there to support the No One Eats Alone **initiative**.

No One Eats Alone encourages students to include one another while they eat lunch. Trump wanted to support this message as part of her anti-bullying position.

Trump would invite young students to take part in "listening sessions" at the White House. In these sessions, students discussed issues they face at school, at home, and with friends.

She told students at the Michigan school that respect, kindness, and compassion toward other people is **essential**.

Trump's anti-bullying campaign formally launched in May 2018. The project was called Be Best. It focused on the health and well-being of America's children.

Be Best had three target areas of concern. The first was children's social and emotional health. The second was social media and the **negative** effects of people's online behavior. And the third was drug **abuse** among young people or their parents.

Be Best supported organizations that address these issues. The project also aimed to educate children and adults about how to look after themselves and others.

> "It is never OK when a 12-year-old girl or boy is mocked, bullied, or attacked. It is terrible when that happens on the playground. And it is absolutely unacceptable when it is done by someone with no name hiding on the internet."

Trump believed young people face **unique** challenges growing up in the modern world. Social media, she claimed, can help people feel less alone. But it can also be a way to

In her speech unveiling Be Best, Trump called on adults to support children's social, emotional, and physical health.

hurt people. Trump wanted Be Best to teach children to "choose their words wisely." She wanted people to learn to express and manage their emotions in a positive way.

CHAPTER 8

BREAKING THE MOLD

Like most political figures, Trump was a subject of public opinion. A January 2018 poll indicated that 47 percent of Americans approved of her. In October 2018, the US public was polled again. This poll showed that Trump's approval had risen to 54 percent.

In some ways, Trump broke the mold of a traditional First Lady. Individuals in this role were known to defend and support their partners no matter what. But Trump wasn't afraid to openly disagree with her husband. Trump also did not attend many events with the president. When she did, she sometimes traveled separately from him.

Trump's air of independence from the president was unusual. One researcher described the behavior as somewhat **feminist**. Whatever people thought of her, Trump had made the role of First Lady her own.

 We have to find a better way to talk to each other, to disagree with each other, to respect each other.

"It's a lot of responsibility . . . to be married to a man like my husband," Trump said. "I need to be quick, smart, and intelligent."

CHAPTER 9

DREAMS ACHIEVED

Being the First Lady wasn't always easy for Trump. But she considered challenges as part of the job. She described life in the White House as busy but exciting.

Trump's work as First Lady aimed to help children manage the hardships of modern life. And her efforts even moved beyond the United States. In October 2018, Trump took the Be Best **initiative** to Africa.

On the trip, Trump visited several countries, including Ghana, Kenya, and Malawi. In Malawi, Trump met with the nation's First Lady, Gertrude Mutharika. The two women discussed the importance of children's education. Trump also **donated** resources to schools that she visited.

Trump grew up dreaming of a life beyond her small town in central Europe. And her dream came true.

 I want our children in this country, and all around the world, to live a beautiful life, to be safe and secure.

Trump became a model, **entrepreneur**, and famous political figure. In her own quiet manner, Trump commands attention across the world.

Trump visited an orphanage in Kenya during her 2018 trip to Africa.

TIMELINE

1970

On April 26, Melanija Knavs is born in what is now Slovenia. She later changes her name to Melania Knauss.

1996

Knauss moves to New York City to model with the agency ID Models.

2005

Knauss marries Donald Trump in Palm Beach, Florida.

1992

Knauss wins second place in the Look of the Year Contest for the Slovenian magazine *Jana*.

2006

Trump gives birth to a son, Barron, in March.

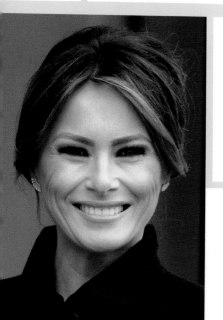

2010

Trump launches the successful jewelry collection Melania Timepieces & Jewelry.

October 2017

Trump visits a middle school in Michigan to support the No One Eats Alone initiative.

October 2018

Trump visits Ghana, Kenya, and other African countries to discuss Be Best initiatives abroad.

January 2017

Donald Trump becomes US president and Melania Trump becomes First Lady.

May 2018

Trump formally launches the anti-bullying campaign Be Best.

GLOSSARY

abuse—the incorrect or improper use of something.

architecture—the art of planning and designing buildings.

communist—relating to a social and economic system in which everything is owned by the government and given to the people as needed.

demoralize—to cause someone to lose hope or confidence.

disciplined—having self-control.

donate—to give.

entrepreneur—one who organizes, manages, and accepts the risks of a business or an enterprise.

essential—very important or necessary.

feminist—relating to feminism, the belief that women and men should have equal rights and opportunities.

immigrate—to enter another country to live.

inauguration (ih-naw-gyuh-RAY-shuhn)—a ceremony in which a person is sworn into a political office.

initial—occurring at or marking the beginning.

initiative—a plan or program that is intended to solve a problem.

intimidate—to frighten.

negative—bad or hurtful.

priority—the condition of coming before others, as in order or importance.

skyscraper—a very tall building.

textile—a woven fabric or cloth.

unique (yoo-NEEK)—being the only one of its kind.

upheaval—a period of great change or disorder.

ONLINE RESOURCES

Booklinks
NONFICTION NETWORK
FREE! ONLINE NONFICTION RESOURCES

To learn more about Melania Trump, please visit **abdobooklinks.com** or scan this QR code. These links are routinely monitored and updated to provide the most current information available.

INDEX